MEMORY OF FIRE

Memory of Fire is a collection of poems composed by Clare Maynard while travelling between Wales and Germany and in other parts of Europe over a period of ten years. The majority of the poems were written in cafés in Berlin during the winter months, drawing on past memories.

The collection captures the different atmospheres of rural and urban landscapes, evoking both myth and the historical changes experienced by those who live inside and outside of the towns and cities, also how countryside and city can represent transient and static cultures, some of them remaining unchanged throughout the years.

The Berlin poems evoke the ravages of a volatile history which can still be seen in the buildings and urban landscape. Where they touch on the political, the poems address the often harsh conditions of rural life hidden within the idyllic viewpoint, or contrast it to the modernism of the city. The more personal poems, relating to friendships or family, evoke the sense of loss when paths divide. The roots of many of the poems can be found in meeting people like herself while on her journeys, people of both of past and present diasporas.

Dear Hilaire
happy reading
with much love
Clare :) x

MEMORY OF FIRE

CLARE MAYNARD

For Lee and Simon

CONTENTS

POEMS

2002 - 2012

MEMORY OF FIRE

The Etruscans saw flocks of birds as auguries

They are the mechanism of our sky,
our wheel of the mind
turning ahead of us
wingspan wide.

Some are shy and curling.
Others are
arrows through
the clouds.

We sit on our haunches
in the sweltering heat
watching each wing beat
into a New Year.

Was it just the weather pattern?
Is it the harbinger of the storm,
the ruin of crops?

Or the end of our world as it was known
before the destruction of our words?

ENGLAND

A single star hangs beneath a bright moon,
a circus tent sky
and a fading sun on
frost-filled fields.

It seems as though
the whole world
were lifted high
into the dusk.

The island rises
from the darkening sea
and each home county
unfolds into the wintery night.

VITERBO

*During Mussolini's regime the river running through the
city of Viterbo, Italy, was filled in with concrete and
turned into a road*

The priest walks in airy light
in the fine piazza.

The dark stone
buildings surround
a busy square of sun.

Flags are raised in the town
and all the people walk,
run and skip
down its dark alleys
of cobbled stone
to laugh or cry
as the days pass
with the pain of knowing
that the river
was now a road.

THE TOWER

For Simon

Echoes
as though
I am inside a large metal bell
for seven days
forever.

My body, my legs ache.
I only dare to breathe
and later rise.

And I walk with the red rose
to the tower.

Stairs twist far into the clouds,
extracted from the mind's eye.

On this northern plain
of marshland
and cool winds
as though the first tower
had been invented here.

Your winding mind did
what it did.

You laughed a lot,
a distant laugh,
hollow from the heights,
and as you reached out one day
to touch the angel at my shoulder,
a play of golden light
lit your smile.

Now you are gone into the dark
and I lay the rose
on the first step.

ON THE BRIDGE

Christmas trees burn,
fireworks spin ...
in light and sparks.

On the bridge people gather,
ready to rise and fall.

At Silvester
they brush off sparks,
their eyes aflame,
as the dark wolf of the soul
creeps into a New Year.

SUMMER

In the oak hall
I see you again.

You hand me
a wooden bowl

of summer
herbs.

I scoop them up,
the scent of them,

the leaves fall to the floor.

After the rain
the cool wind

carries forth

the peacock's
echoing call.

THE HONEY WALK

A queen bee breeding station, Wales

The bees invite me
to their world
in the deep green valley
impressed on my memory
as the seasons unfold.

My feet on the hot dry road.
Air cools
low in the valley.
Near the bridge
in the shade of trees
complex hives
stand still.

At the bee station entrance
there is a soft grassy yard.
Old sheds lean upon each other.
A weighing scales stands
near abandoned cars.

In the old porch sunlight catches jars,
stacked pyramid-style.
Golden glass spills light.

This honey is the currency for their work.
I wonder are the flowers
kept in their memory?

Dedicated to Andrew Shaw,
may he rest in gentle light

THE SCENT OF RAIN

Normandy, France

Clouds sweep over the land.
A grey curtain rains down.

We live by the weather,
its moods seep into our bones
and deliver each day
with the scent of rain.
The sun's heat
creaks through the window frame.
Cut logs lie moss-covered in the yard,
asleep with junk.

Larch trees in rows
and rain soaked tracks
reflect slivers of light.

A winter cloud bank rises
as rain drops blink
and shatter across the
windscreen.

At last a long blast of spring sun
forms the cloud's voluminous wall
of circus shapes.

This land goes on
as flat as the Fens
anchored into earth's green mantle.

CARDIOGRAM

Heart beat
skips across
the page,
each graphite mark
a deeper dip
than the last,
falling into
white noise.

INTO THE WEST

Journeying into the dark West
and down into
under
land.

Passion and joy reside
amongst the trees
of mischief.

There is a promise of delight,
all souls are kind,
they wait with their dogs
to comfort
day and night.

THE HARLECH STONES

He bobs in the distance
above the tall grass,
waving hair, a contrast
black as the mountains
behind him.

Today he is surveyor
on this wild hill
overlooking a distant castle
and a sprinkle of a town.

The only colour is the red dot
of his coat which moves
within the mist.

He reaches
the stone
and I strain my eyes to watch
the way he turns to
look closer, notebook in hand.

I am wrapped in the distant warmth
in the shell of the car.

Coat-blown he returns,
brings the breeze in,
silently passes the book to me.
I agree it is a fine and bold stone.

Later I study these lines.
I push my finger around the inky shape
and when he is away
I am reminded of the ancient past
and of him
drawn into the future.

MANANNÁN

One winter's night I read
the future weather
for my friend
to help her distant journey to an island.

I hovered as a bird would
over the most beautiful gem in the sea.

I was eye to eye with birds
for time was slow enough.

I saw glittering
shores and the sun
and I knew it would embrace her.

I awoke laughing
for the first time
since tragedy had buried my spirit
in a dull hole
and then I was urgently advised,
told to seek protection
in the form of some deity.

But in what form?

Grief
is a desert
where sand runs slowly
and sometimes quickly
through the glass.

Then manifested
a large and humorous man,
magnanimous lover
of the ocean and the shores,
a protector of spirits who move
between worlds,
he who helped me laugh again.

His tree is the hawthorn,
bright and sharp with berries.
In the folded bark his green force grows,
gate keeper of souls.

NOTE:

Manannán Mac Lir - a Celtic spirit protector who assists spirits travelling from one world to the next; he visits people by playing practical jokes, changing the weather, or appearing in person to make someone laugh, or encouraging astral voyages. He is associated with the sea and often islands. People say that they just know when he has visited them during a difficult time. He is associated with Ireland, Wales and the Isle of Man.

IBERIAN SONG

We meet
and pass the time of day
on dusty roads.
We dance in evening light.
We walk and then run
into the gold rush.

Our fathers dreamt of stars
at Córdoba and Granada.
They climbed the university stairs
and danced along the irrigation lines.

Now the mountain passes
and the sunlit green hills
are a guide to wanderers.

BERLIN NIGHTS

In a bright store
a woman stands tall
with a small dog,
its quick paws skid to and fro.

The sound of a sled
sings in the solid air,
snow on the ground.

Trees dark
against the pale façades
of buildings
where squares of
neon light float
from a window.

Two figures glide
along the icy boulevard,
their breath marks the air like a spectre,
their dark coats absorb the night.

GLYNDWR

Bring me nothing for I have no slaves.
A gentle horse
and a ring of oaks
are my abode.

Sunlight and shadows on a carpet of green,
a forest floor of crackling leaves.
Head bowed upon the mountain,
I watch my people
in transition.

The old walk into autumn,
their eyes aflame with passion.
The young are fire flowers
who speak the old language
on the mountain's edge.

FRANCE

Poplar trees skim the horizon,
neon strips of light
cut through the nightscape,
circling around the church spires
and over the Lille by-pass.

Christmas debris litters the streets,
restaurants are alive with
the post-Christmas meetings
of those who wish company
from each other still.

Again I see that lonely house in the field,
the long track,
the Citroen parked there.

I imagine a scenario
where wife or husband
are always home late.

EAST

On reading W G Sebald's 'The Rings of Saturn'

We were a shining jewel then,
we loved the great adventure
on vast beaches
of other sea sounds.

We laughed under boughs of golden apples
while the calm of the sprinkled lawn
caught the petals
from the blossomed tree
as
they
fell.

We had lived
and some died young,
a picture of them
hung like a quiet sheet of song.

The dogs waited in the morning mist
while still farm machines dripped oil.

In the cool of the morning we would wake
to larks in the fields.
We cupped our hands around the soil,
around the nights.
We had seen our own perfection,
a fortress made from stones
pulled from the beach.

This was our domain,
our dream,
luminescent as silver fish
skim and spin.

A storm arrived,
it bounced grey and silver
across the land.

And our hearts, as dull as stone,
weighed heavy in the night.

I waited for one year.
The hedgerows played a joyous song
while our souls were torn
under the wide sky.

II

Your return:
we spoke of the dysfunction of our lives,
our bubbles,
these ideal homes,
how they only offered comfort
to the blankness of the morning.

And among the chaos of this end
there were days of sweltering sun,
your cynical jokes rang true,
as dry as the hay strewn steps
that we climbed.

BRANDENBURG

Fruit-tree lined road, long and sandy,
reminds me of Norfolk land.

A horse walks through the woods
as lightning strikes a silver birch.

FIELDFARES

Our footprints climb
contours of pure white hills,
follow sled tracks,
near smaller prints
which weave their way
through ours.

Trees are startled
by winter's pale sunlight,
their branches splayed in welcome.

We move into untouched snow
where blue light reflects
millions of tiny ice trees
blown across the surface.

Dark boundaries sketch the horizon,
a release to the sky.

A flurry of soft brown birds rises.
My friend explains
in a white breath-cloud:
"Fieldfares,
smaller than a mistle-thrush."

Her gloved hands float in the air
as she describes their size.

Along an ice ridge
sheep yellow eyes
greet us as the cold bites deep
into the hollow psyche;
under fur and coats
it numbs toes and fingers,
pulls us toward home and heat
and into the long thaw.

Gateway Café

The gateway east to west,
music slow and easy,
a dream
caught in time.

People drift into corners
slightly ruffled from the cold.

A white dove flies
from the darkness of a photograph.
Outside the plants on the Platz
are lit like snowflakes falling.

Drift in, to write, read or talk,
life takes on a slow pace as
weak sunlight
plays
on the windows,
cars skim past,
the city sings,
a grainy film flickering.

The end of an era.
Tears are in the written word,
a revolution passed,
people gave out flowers on the street
and the Platz fountain sparkled throughout
the night.

GWYDIR

*It is said that there is a ghost at Gwydir,
a medieval castle in North Wales*

This place sits deep in the valley.
The peacocks strut in the sun,
the blue-green rays of their chests
shimmer in the light.

The wooden panels of this ancient house
creak through the night;
the oak stairs shine,
worn by generations.

Through leaded windows
candlelight flickers.
She sits on the old window seat,
the warm night air circles
with beautiful moths,
her green velvet dress
gathered around her.
Beyond the lawn and the box bush
a peacock screeches its eerie arrival.

THE LONG LAKE

Moravia, the Czech Republic

Through dust and sun soaked windows
there is a view to the long lake.

Figures pass in winter coats,
hands deep in pockets,
faces sketched in snow.

Branches bent
form snow dens in the forest
and cross-country skiers
leave their easy marks on
this rich and fragrant earth
trodden by centuries
of toil and travel.

Winter darkness lifts
and light spills along the ice.

It is a distant dream
as summer comes
to this place.

STRATA FLORIDA

A Cistercian abbey in mid-Wales

I sat on the moss-covered wall
reading inscriptions in stone for
those long lives in sackcloth
and terrifying island winters.

Their thoughts, on survival,
on sheep and mead,
and a man leading a black horse,
passed me by.

Only the vast sky and
only the grass.

The rain lashed high windows
stained with the love of God.

Woodland paths lead to
flowered glades
and a stick cracks underfoot,
the only sound for miles
as leaves fall down
to cover the ground.

SILVER BIRCHES

After the overland of France
and into Germany
I awoke
heavy, deep with dreaming.

Silver birches flicker white
past the window,
a film
caught on a reel.

I see them in the city,
pale ghosts in courtyards,
in parks,
reminders of journeys
past.

The Passage Through

Heat permeates this road
through the valley.
I explore as a child would,
no one can see me.

The sun's heat plays on my skin
like wildfire,
it seeps into my bones
from the soles of my feet.

The horse in the field hangs his heavy head,
his gaze a gleaming eye;
he knows I am weaker than he
and he watches with wonder and caution.

Tall houses, the bridge and the river,
the red post-box
embedded in the stone wall.

The forest lies in the distance,
its hidden ruins desolate yet
inviting in the gloom.

The green cloak of a wet day
on the bark and stones,
an emerald world.

I recall other valleys
on the map,
unexplored.
And I bend to collect some warm grit,
let my hand absorb
its heat.
I let it fall through my grasp.

I turn to the cool of the house.
a point of reference,
a slow walk through
the village,
the routine of each day,

and the arrival,
that very ending
which is so elusive.

LEAVES

Swept along by a swishing broom
on the street
in this Romanian town
outside the white hospital

the wind catches them
as they change and curl.

A mark of her years,
a black headscarf
hides her hair.

Sunlight streams through the arches,
a child meanders,
lost under the high ceilings
in this temple of work.

II

The corn blows across the plain,
the travelling workers
seek their daily bread
and dance in the city park at night.

Lives run in circles
even when free.

Lightning Source UK Ltd.
Milton Keynes UK
UKOW03f1000050114

224003UK00001B/2/P